MAKE

IT

HAPPEN

To Crissy
My best life starts with you.

CONTENTS

CONTENTS

CONTENTS

PART V

The Secret to Success

ACKNOWLEDGEMENTS

This book is my gift to the numerous people in my life who have taught me, guided me, loved me and supported me wholeheartedly in even my craziest of dreams.

I thank You, Lord, for Your abundant blessings and daily grace. All things are possible in Jesus' name.

Rosetta, Mario Sr., Lorena, Todd, Ryan, Linda, Steven, Tianna, Nicholas, Lisa, Jason, Catherine and Cristina – family isn't everything; it's the only thing. I love you.

To Angelo, Joanne, Mark, Krista, Evan, Jasper, David, Tanis, Lola, Leo and Anthony – I am so grateful to have felt your warm welcome since day one.

My dear extended family and friends – thank you for helping to shape me into who I am today. I cherish all of the unique memories I share with each of you.

Father Ron Ambeault – I truly appreciate your spiritual guidance and friendship. Thank you for always encouraging me

ACKNOWLEDGEMENTS

in all of life's journeys.

To the original crew at Rome's Independent Grocer – it was an honor growing up amongst all of you.

My wonderful "kids" – the students with whom I've spent so much time over the years – I've learned the most valuable life lessons from you.

To my numerous colleagues at the Huron-Superior Catholic District School Board – I am constantly amazed by the work you do for our students.

Heartfelt thanks to Rose Calcafuoco, my high school English teacher and editor of this book. I look up to you now the same way I did as a 14-year-old boy at SBSS where you brought my love of reading and writing to a whole new level. Thank you for your guidance – then, now and always.

I have been blessed to learn from the greatest instructors known to mankind. I get such an awesome feeling whenever I look back at my educational experiences. To my teachers from Holy Family, St. Basil Secondary, Algoma University and Nipissing University – thank you for igniting in me a passion to mentor and help others.

I am forever grateful for the knowledge and wisdom instilled in me by my coach and motivational friend Tony Gaskins, Jr. I promise to give tirelessly to others the way you have given to me.

ACKNOWLEDGEMENTS

My life changed drastically in 2009 when I met Michael Graziadei and embarked upon my first journey into the world of entertainment. Graz, you've been the catalyst of everything I've become. Thank you for showing me a whole new world. It is my honor and privilege to call you my friend and my brother.

To Greg Rikaart, Joshua Morrow, Christian LeBlanc, Billy Miller and Thad Luckinbill – thank you for the love and support you have shown my family and me over the years. Some of my fondest memories to date include our awesome times together in the Soo. It is a blessing to know each of you.

My brother in Christ, Michael Conley – I will forever be thankful to the "roses" for bringing our paths together. Thank you for showing me what it means to be a man of faith in action.

To Bret Michaels, one of the hardest working men I know – your passion and zest for life are contagious. Thank you for inspiring me to "live fully and tread lightly." Rock on, my brother. Rock on.

And last but not least, to *you*, the person reading this book right now – thank you for picking up a copy and giving me a chance to speak into your life. I am humbled and grateful for the opportunity.

INTRODUCTION
Your Best Life Awaits

In my first 30 years on God's green earth, I've watched many people climb the ladder of success. From childhood to young adulthood, I served as the perfect spectator in this game we call life, a sort of cheerleader for those around me who seemed to always get what they wanted. Make no mistake about it – I loved every minute of growing up in Sault Ste. Marie, Canada. I've always had a great family, great friends and great teachers. Life couldn't get any better.

Or could it?

You see, despite my happiness, there was always a yearning deep inside of me that said, "Mario, there are more blessings waiting for you." A little voice that never ceased to whisper, "You are meant for more."

By picking up this book, I know that a similar voice exists inside of you.

In fact, I've come to the conclusion that no matter

where we are in life, how high we are at any given moment, there is always a desire for more. A healthy desire. A desire that says, "I'm living a good life, but I want to live my *best* life." That's where this guide comes into play.

Within the pages of this book are stories, anecdotes and life lessons for anyone who is looking to bring his or her life to the next level. As you read through, remember that the title of this book focuses on living *your* best life. Not your friend's life, not your co-worker's life, not your boss' life. *Your* life. There's no competition. It's okay to focus on you. It's not selfish; it's empowering. And it's what you need to do to truly give yourself the life you've always wanted.

As you navigate through the guide, you'll notice that some of the stories and examples remind you of people you know in your own life. In some cases, it may sound like I'm talking directly about you. I assure you, it's nothing personal. The people and situations depicted in this guide will sound familiar because they are people that we all know and situations that we have all experienced.

Open yourself up to face the uncomfortable, necessary truths communicated across these pages. Think carefully about the lessons that can be learned in each chapter. Relate this book to your life and consider the advice being given. It will not only elevate your life but the lives of those around you. As you learn to appreciate and act upon your blessings, you will become a blessing to everyone in your path.

A fire is started by a single spark. It's time to stop making excuses and to start lighting that flame. Make it happen. Your best life awaits.

– Mario J. Rocchetta

MAKE

IT

HAPPEN

PART

I

The Choice is Yours

CHAPTER ONE
Choose Happiness

A long time ago, Abraham Lincoln revealed a profound secret that holds just as true today as the moment he said it: "Most people are as happy as they've decided to be."

Somehow over the course of time, as society evolved and our priorities changed, Honest Abe's words have become lost in the shuffle. Even reading his quote now, it seems overly simplistic. But if you take a moment to let it sink in, there really is no better way to start living your best life than to follow this piece of advice.

Happiness is a choice. It's also a form of courage. For some people, it's actually very difficult to be happy. Life's challenges and difficulties pile up and leave them feeling lost, scared and hopeless. Chances are you've experienced a time where it didn't just rain, it poured. You may be going through a tough situation right now. But whatever challenge you currently face, whatever obstacle is standing in your way, trust me when

I say that it will not be there forever. Even the darkest and stormiest sky will give way to a bright and beautiful sun.

How you will live your life in spite of current difficulties is a choice that you have to make. You need to decide, at the start of each day, just how happy you will be. Don't wake up and leave your mind in neutral. The negativity and misery of others will take your neutral mind and kick it into the wrong gear. You need to blatantly choose happiness ahead of time.

I had a friend in university who was a real downer. Throughout the course of any given day, she'd criticize our school, our classes, the people in our classes – heck, she was even critical of me, now that I think about it. At that time in my life, I was really starting to grow comfortable in my own skin and began realizing what it meant to choose happiness. I would intentionally walk into school each day with a smile on my face and a spring in my step. I thought to myself, "Not only am I choosing to be happy, but I'm going to make her happy as well."

It took me three years to realize that I was fighting a losing battle. Day in and day out, I exhausted myself trying to make her happy. The result was an ugly end to our friendship due to years of bitter feelings and wasted time.

In those moments, I could simply never understand why she was so miserable. Ten years later, I still can't understand what her problem was. It took me a long time to learn what I'm telling you right now – be happy for your sake, not for the sake of anyone else. Don't make it your duty to try and spread your happiness to those around you. Some people don't even want to be happy. Instead, choose your own happiness and let it radiate to others. Those who choose happiness in their own lives will experience your joy and vice-versa.

To live your best life, you absolutely need to choose happiness. Some days will be more difficult than others. We all have moments of sadness, self-pity and grief. If, however, you program your mind to choose happiness, your good days will numerously outweigh your bad days. Your light will shine and attract the right people into your life.

Several years ago, I was doing some run-of-the-mill writing for my employer at an online soap opera blog. I admit that I was in a bit of a rut. My writing wasn't taking me where I wanted to go and I was starting to develop a real foul outlook toward my work. Instead of falling prey to my thoughts, I re-programmed my mind to recognize the blessing of that current day. I thought to myself, "I am excited to be alive at this moment. I am excited to write for this online magazine, even though it isn't paying me much or getting me to Hollywood as quickly as I had hoped. I am happy for this opportunity."

In the throes of my self-pity and despair, I was seconds

away from walking away from it all. I literally felt like it was time to give up. The writing, my dream to work in the entertainment industry – I was ready to say goodbye to it all and never look back. But once I consciously reprogrammed my thoughts and blatantly chose happiness, I continued to write my current story.

That very night, my phone rang. On the other end of the line was a Hollywood publicist who offered me, right then and there, my best star interview to date. Not only that, but this publicist and I engaged in an hour-long personal phone chat (something very rare in the business) and have been close friends and spiritual brothers ever since. This phone call also led me to my first red-carpet experience at the Daytime Emmy Awards – a moment I had dreamed about since I was a little boy.

Had I not chosen happiness that night several years ago, just hours before the phone call that changed my life, there's no telling where my path would have led. If I had allowed my happiness to be sucked dry by the everyday grind, I would never have made myself available for the call that altered my destiny. What a shame it would have been to miss out on my best life because of a few moments of sadness and self-pity!

Starting right now, have the courage to be happy in

your life. The choice to make this happen will open doors for you that you have only dreamed could exist. Being happy looks good on you. If you want to live your best life, the simplest and most effective way to begin is by choosing happiness at the start of each day.

CHAPTER TWO
Choose Kindness

Once you've decided to make happiness a daily choice, the next step to living your best life is to choose kindness. Choosing kindness is not simply "being nice." It's about exemplifying a generous and compassionate spirit with others. Kindness is about letting your heart, not your mind, take precedence in your relationships.

Last year, I had the opportunity to teach a wonderful group of sixth- and seventh-graders. In one of our Language Arts novel studies, my students and I came across an inspirational quote from author and motivational speaker Dr. Wayne Dyer: "When given the choice between being right or being kind, choose kind." It still gives me goosebumps when I think about how quickly these children were able to decipher the meaning of Dr. Dyer's words.

If a group of young people can understand kindness, why do so many adults struggle with it? Granted, children have their own share of unkind moments, but I feel it's safe to say that adults are much more guilty of such transgressions. As we grow older, we learn that being *right* is the best way to get rewarded in life. After all, how many people receive a university scholarship for being kind? Or a raise at work for being generous? More often than not, intelligence takes precedence in our world.

You, however, have the power to change the direction of this flailing ship. You have the ability, in your own life, to choose kindness. If you truly want to live your best life, it is absolutely mandatory that you prioritize being kind ahead of being right.

When I meet people for the first time, like new co-workers, I make it a point to ask them a lot of questions about themselves, their lives and their families. With a kind spirit, I show a genuine appreciation for these new people in my life whom I've been blessed to meet. Even if these people and I engage in a topic where they are clearly messing up some facts, if it's unimportant and no one is getting hurt, I'll just let it go. I don't have time to be a know-it-all and correct people. I'm more interested in being kind and compassionate.

Give this a try – the next time you meet a new acquaintance, remind yourself that it's more important to be kind than right. The next time you hear someone state a wrong fact and it's totally innocent, let go of your need to correct him or her. Let go of your need to impress anyone with your knowledge of any given subject. When your time on Earth comes to an end, no one will remember how smart you were. Instead, people will remember how you made them feel. Your kindness will create and establish your legacy for years to come.

Simply be kind. Genuinely enjoy the moment. Know that your kindness is winning you more favor with the people around you than any level of intelligence ever could. If you want to live your best life and have more people on your side, being kind will always leave a more lasting impression than being right.

CHAPTER THREE

Choose Forgiveness

It's been said that holding onto a grudge is like sitting in a rocking chair – it gives you something to do but you never go anywhere. I prefer to use the analogy that holding onto a grudge is like running on a treadmill. You can kick your speed into high gear and even build up a great sweat, but, at the end of your run, you're still physically in the same place. You haven't moved. So, too, is the case with being unable to forgive someone who has done you wrong.

If you're human, you've experienced at least one situation in your life where someone in your inner circle has wronged you. A time where you've been hurt, betrayed or mistreated by a loved one. Chances are, you're thinking of that person and that situation at this very moment. It's like you're on that treadmill, dedicating a lot of sweat and energy to the cause but, ultimately, running in the same place.

You need to choose forgiveness right now. How can

you choose happiness and kindness if you refuse to let go of your anger toward someone who has hurt you? I promise you, it's impossible. Happiness, kindness and forgiveness need to come together in your life so that you can bring your purpose to the next level. If you are completely serious about living your best life, there's absolutely no time to hold onto grudges.

I once had a friend who always seemed to be there for me through thick and thin. Our friendship grew over the years into a brotherhood. At the time, I used to think that this guy was a flawless, close friend. He supported me in my dreams. In fact, he was one of the first people to encourage me toward breaking into the entertainment industry as a promoter. He said that he believed in me and that he would stand by my side in all of my ventures.

Then, in one swift betrayal, he was gone.

I'll never forget the day I realized that I had been blind-sided. While building my brand as a promoter with stars from *The Young and the Restless*, I was also working on a project in the field of teaching. As the story goes, this friend went ahead, without my knowledge, and started a similar project. His plan of action was identical to what I had been working on except his plan had absolutely zero room for me. When I phoned him to ask about the project, he offered no excuse. I asked him how he could go ahead and betray me in such a way. I was so

14

confused. He told me it was simply his time to shine and then had a few other words for me that made me feel about the size of an ant. He treated the situation as if it were merely a case of, "You snooze, you lose."

The two of us were never friends again. As a matter of fact, things only got worse. Month after month, year after year, I stewed over the events that took place. I blamed him for everything under the sun. I thought he was a monster for turning his back on me. I vowed to never forgive him for the pain and stress he put me through.

With time, I realized that it actually wasn't *he* who was causing any pain or stress in my life. It was *I* who was doing the damage. Not only was my mind always heavy but my tongue was constantly on fire with venomous, spiteful words of anger toward him. Truth be told, I became the monster I was trying to fight.

Looking back, what was it all worth? His project had fallen through, anyway. Even if it hadn't, it still wouldn't have changed the fact that the damage was done. At the time, I was so consumed by my inability to forgive that I could not see the blessing behind the conflict. The blessing was that someone who was not good for me had been removed from my life.

I tell you this story because I know that you've had friends just like this. People who have hurt you in the past, maybe even multiple times. Don't continue to hold onto the pain. Recognize that these individuals who have hurt you are simply not meant to be in your life. They may have been meant for you in the past, but, I assure you, their season is over. It's time for your show to move on.

People who have a genuine place in your world will not cause so much damage to you that it leaves emotional or physical scars. If the pain they inflict on you is constantly lingering then that's a sign that you need to let them go. Whatever you are holding onto right now, at this very moment, let it go. Don't just pretend to let it go; let it go with all of your heart and soul.

Confidently and assuredly, move away from the source of your pain and sadness. This may all sound easier said than done, but, I promise you, the more you practice forgiveness, the more quickly you will see how easy it is to let go and move on. Forgiveness is not about letting anybody "off the hook." Forgiveness actually has nothing to do with the person you are forgiving. It does, however, have everything to do with *you*.

If you want to live your best life, you cannot carry the heavy burden of a grudge. You cannot climb to the top of the mountain with unnecessary weight on your back. It's time to lighten your load. Forgive. Feel the burden lift off of your shoulders. In doing so, recognize that the past is now officially over. You are free to move away from any disappointment you have ever known. You are now free to live your best life.

PART
II

Think Straight

CHAPTER FOUR
Think Like a Star

Once you've started to fill your life with happiness, kindness and forgiveness, it will be just a matter of time before you notice an abundance of blessings coming into your world. This is no coincidence; it's the result of having an open mind and a forgiving heart.

With this fresh mindset and revitalized outlook on life, you will notice the doors that were once closed are now starting to open. The opportunities for which you've been praying are lining up for you and your family at just the right time.

When I started my foray into the world of entertainment, I had no idea just how much my life would change. Here I was, in my mid-to-late 20s, living the life I had always wanted, sharing the stage with some of my favorite actors in the world. It was a dream come true. I pinched myself often to ensure that it was real. I was so excited and so ready for the glittering spotlight to shine in my direction.

But, as the saying goes, "All that glitters isn't gold."

Don't get me wrong. The events I've hosted and experiences I've had up to this point have been everything I had always dreamed about and more. A lot more, unfortunately, than I had bargained for.

It didn't take me long to realize that with a very big spotlight comes a very big shadow. The more successful I grew in my work and the more I sincerely attempted to share these gifts with my entire community, the more I felt the heat. I felt the awkward silences grow between me and some individuals who I used to know. I heard the chit-chat around town. I read the vicious comments on local news sites of anonymous people posting disgusting personal attacks on my character.

Why was this happening? Didn't people want to celebrate with me? Weren't people excited for me? Wasn't I doing enough to make my critics happy?

I was really bothered by these questions, so I asked them to a friend in the business who I knew had experienced something similar. He replied, very simply, "These people will never be happy. That's why they're critics."

He then looked me in the eye and said, "Mario, you've got to start thinking like a star."

I tell you, my life has never been better since I heeded this advice. Not just my life as a promoter but my life as a teacher and my life as a human being.

What does it mean to think like a star? It means living your life in such a way that you do what makes you happy without feeling the need to entertain the negative opinions of others. I don't mean walking around thinking that you're better than everyone else. Simply put, thinking like a star means coming to the realization that whatever your critics say about you has no bearing on your worth.

Anyone can tell you that what you're doing is no good. In fact, a lot of people *will* tell you this. They will judge you and question you about your life and the choices you make. A lot of the time, you won't even know that they're doing this because it will all happen behind your back.

Don't sweat it. When you think like a star, you don't waste your time and positive energy on negative people. Thinking like a star means recognizing that people talk behind your back because you are out in front. You are a leader and a visionary. You're doing things that other people only wish they could do. They'll make it look like you're not doing anything special and that what you're doing is easy. But I assure you, if it was easy, everyone would be doing it.

Stay focused and keep your thoughts on the right track. What other people think of you is none of your business! The simple fact of the matter is this – not everyone wants to see you succeed. Some of your friends, and maybe even some people in your family, want to see you live nothing more than a normal, average life. They find it offensive if you seek better for yourself. Perhaps they are stuck in their current situation and want you to be, too. But do not let this sad truth keep you from fulfilling your dreams. Now is the time for you to accept the fact that some people will never celebrate your gifts or your accomplishments. Now is the time for you to start thinking like a star!

CHAPTER FIVE
Think Like a Winner

Winners don't win because they're lucky. Winners win because they recognize the preparation and hard work needed to be victorious. Thinking like a star allows you the freedom to break free from even your harshest critics, but it's thinking like a winner that will prepare you for victory at the start of each day.

I've always wanted two things out of my life – to teach others and to entertain others. Becoming a teacher, though it involved a lot of hard work, was simple in the sense that my journey was easily mapped out. There's a certain amount of schooling you need, and certain courses you need to take, in order to obtain a Bachelor of Education. On the other hand, learning to become a promoter of live events featuring the biggest stars from *The Young and the Restless* doesn't really come with a user manual!

I'll never forget my initial attempt at securing a live

soap opera event in my hometown of Sault Ste. Marie. I made my first phone call to a Hollywood agent with nothing to back me up other than my passion to enter the business and my will to prove all doubters wrong.

If there existed a manual on how to be a promoter, perhaps it would have saved me from the embarrassment that was to follow.

My first call to Hollywood lasted a whopping twenty seconds and resulted in nothing more than me having the phone slammed down in my face.

It was in this moment of adversity, though, that I learned what it means to think like a winner. Contrary to what you've read as a child on your teacher's motivational posters, you need a lot more than just passion to achieve victory. You also need a plan of action.

After the hang-up incident, it took me quite some time to get a business plan together. I was determined that my next phone call would bring me success. I still had almost no clue as to what I was doing, but that's where my passion served useful. It pushed me to research, study and prepare for the road ahead. I recall being wide awake on a random summer night at 4 AM bouncing ideas around with my sister Lisa, one of the only people at the time who believed that I had what it took to accomplish this dream.

Looking back, I know that it was because of this winning mindset that I rocked my next phone call to Hollywood. I had done my homework and was set up for victory. I carried out my action plan to a tee. I was thinking like a winner. Tied in with my passion to succeed, I refused to lose and the rest is history.

What is the next step that you've been itching to take in your own life? Getting a promotion at work? Quitting your job and starting a new one? Learning something new, perhaps a musical instrument or a new language? Whatever your aspirations are, determine right now what's really holding you back from accomplishing these goals. If people are critical, ignore them and move on. But if it's your own lack of planning that's tying you down, recognize that *you* are the only person who can change this.

If you don't know how to start your winning plan of attack, I recommend hiring a life coach to help bring you to the next level. A life coach will not only hold you accountable for thinking like a winner, but will help you to devise an action plan that will take your purpose further than you could have ever imagined. If you're in need of a gentle push from someone who truly wants to help you succeed, hiring a life coach may be the first step you need to take. Investing in a life coach means directly investing in yourself. Once you've invested in yourself, your possibilities become endless. The dreams which once seemed so far away and were only figments of your imagination are now real and tangible.

What are you waiting for? It's time to start winning right now. Think like a winner and act upon your thoughts. Do the necessary work to bring yourself to the next level. Make it happen. Opportunity doesn't usually come knocking; you need to seek it out. Create your opportunities and create your world. The possibilities are endless and your best life is attainable when you think like a winner.

CHAPTER SIX

Think Like a Champion

What's the difference between being a winner and being a champion? With a solid action plan and the determination to bring it to fruition, victory is inevitably yours for the taking. As a winner, you will achieve your goals and experience an abundance of blessings greater than people who keep their minds stuck in the idle position.

But only a select few winners become champions.

Champions make you want to watch and cheer for them every step of the way. They are compelling and inspirational figures. Their work ethic is contagious.

A champion not only wins but helps others to win, too.

It's been said that the best way to get what you want is to help others get what they want. In other words, if you want to be successful, help others succeed. If you want to make money, help others make money. These are just a few examples of what it means to think like a champion.

When you have the mentality of a champion, you are actually sowing seeds for your purpose in life to grow higher. By helping others to get what they want, you're not only building friendships and a solid social network, but storing up treasures of your own that will no doubt be cashed in at a later time. Call it heavenly favor, good karma or anything else you'd like. The fact is, what goes around comes around. When you are a blessing to others, you will receive an abundance of blessings in return.

I recall once hearing a story about Bret, a professional mountain climber, who was making his way to the top of a peak when a terrible snowstorm hit. The climbing became extremely difficult to the point where Bret didn't know if he and his climbing mates would make it.

As the group struggled to navigate its way, Bret noticed an unknown climber who was passed out along the trail. He and his partners recognized that the man on the ground was close to death. Though Bret stopped, his team continued to climb. "Come on, Bret. Keep up. If you stop and try to help, you may not make it yourself!"

Bret refused to leave the man alone to die. As his team went on without him, Bret stayed back and massaged the stranger's limbs and face to get his blood flowing. With Bret's help, the fallen climber was revived enough to get back on his feet and walk with Bret down the mountain to safety.

When the two men were examined by the doctor, it was no surprise that the fallen climber had severe frostbite and had been on the brink of death. Bret *was* surprised, however, to learn that he, too, was showing signs of frostbite.

"When you stopped to massage this man's limbs, you luckily increased the circulation in your own body," said the doctor. "If you didn't stop to help, you likely wouldn't have made it much further up the mountain before succumbing to frostbite, yourself."

What is *your* focus as you climb up the mountain to success? When you finally get to the top, who is up there to share in the moment with you? Do you see yourself alone in victory? Or are you thinking like a champion and envisioning the ways in which you'll help others climb alongside with you? Remember – when you help others win, you are elevating yourself to a level higher than you could ever reach while climbing solo. It's a level at which you can, undoubtedly, live your best life.

PART
III

Take Inventory

CHAPTER SEVEN

Assess Your Friends

It's often said that friends are the family you choose for yourself. I know someone who quotes this phrase all the time. When Facebook started to become popular, she'd post inspirational status updates about friendship and boast about how much fun she and her friends were always having together. Her display pictures would change daily as she'd rotate through her friend roster and show them off, one at a time.

This all seems fine and dandy except for one important detail that conspicuously never gets published on Facebook – all of these friends actually hate each other. In the public forum of social networking, everything comes across as peachy-keen. But anyone who truly knows this group of friends knows that they privately talk trash about one another. It's all one big show.

The unfortunate thing is that I'm not talking about a group of high school students. These are grown women and men who seem to only stick together just so they can one-up each other. They claim to like one another but actually talk trash and share secrets behind closed doors.

Take a look at your life. It's time to assess the people that you allow to be in your inventory. If these people are spreading secrets about others when they're not around, it's likely that they're spreading secrets about you when you're not around.

Remember, friends are the family you choose for yourself. If a friend is in your life it's because you've chosen to have him or her fill that spot. Do your friends help you or hinder you? If they are hindering you in any way, it's time to move them out of your inventory.

The problem nowadays is that a lot of people have such a wide variety of friendships stemming from so many places. Friends you've known your whole life, friends from your workplace, friends from the gym, friends on Facebook, followers on Twitter – the supply is endless. Equipped with the latest technology, we cultivate these friendships 24/7.

Having friends in all these areas isn't a bad thing in and of itself. In fact, studies show that having a large social network can lead to greater feelings of life satisfaction and self-worth. The danger comes when we start to mistake who our true friends are. With so many wolves dressed in sheep's clothing, it's easy to place your trust in the wrong people.

I wholeheartedly encourage you, right now, to take an honest and sincere inventory of your friendships. Let go of the need to have more friends, and instead, preoccupy yourself with keeping close only those who help to better your life.

Consider this exercise in friend selection as the equivalent to cutting your front lawn. If your grass is left to grow wild and out of control, there's no telling what sort of snakes are slithering around your territory. Take control of your life today and cut your grass low. As rapper Jay-Z says, "When the grass is cut, the snakes will show." You absolutely must reveal the snakes in your life and exterminate them once and for all.

While mowing your lawn, you may also come across a few dead patches of grass. These represent the friendships in your life that were once vibrant and healthy but are no longer alive. To truly repair these areas, you must start by removing the weeds and damaged grass. The same applies to your dead friendships. You must remove these stagnant friends from your life if you hope to plant new seeds down the road.

Some of my best friends are friends that I've had since kindergarten. We still keep in touch and get together on quite a regular basis. When we sit down together, we love to reminisce and laugh about the good old days. It's like nothing has ever changed between us no matter where our individual paths have led. The important thing, though, is that we still have a common ground and are still creating new memories and experiencing new victories together. This is what makes friendships meaningful in the long run.

Truth be told, I don't have a lot of best friends these days. I love to see a lot of people from my past, and it's great to reminisce with them the way I do with my closest of friends, but I recognize that these people don't have a true spot in my inventory anymore. Their time has passed. I value the role they've played in my life and will forever hold a spot for them in my heart, but they're no longer relevant to my purpose. Life is simply too busy to meaningfully make time for everyone. As we get older, we must love and fondly remember everyone, but only keep close those who still actively contribute to our lives. Unfortunately, all others must go.

Removing friends from your life is not a selfish or callous move. It's simply saying, "I don't have time for people who are not contributing to me being the best person I can be." Few friendships will last the entire series of your life. The majority will play an important role for only one or two seasons.

Parting ways with certain friends doesn't mean that you wish any ill will toward them. You want what's best for you and for them. Your friendship was great while it lasted, but it's run its course. There's nothing more to explore or experience to-gether and that's okay. Recognize the blessing of that friend-ship, how it helped you to grow at a particular time in your life, and then move on. Your best life won't wait while you stick around and hold on to a friendship that has already reached its end.

CHAPTER EIGHT

Assess Your Family

Take a moment to reflect on the following proverb: "An ounce of blood is worth more than a pound of friendship." What does this proverb mean to you? Perhaps reading it has made you think of another, more popular one: "Blood is thicker than water."

Both proverbs communicate the idea that your family members are more valuable than your friends. That your family loves you unconditionally and will stand by you through thick and thin.

Unconditional family love is something I have been lucky enough to experience my whole life. I truly can't imagine a world without my mom and dad, my sisters and brothers-in-law and nieces and nephews. Some of my warmest memories of growing up come from my extended family of aunts and uncles and cousins. There's not a single day that passes where I don't reach out to at least one family member for encouragement or even just a little bit of small talk. My family keeps me going.

Perhaps reading about the bond I have with my family reminds you of the closeness that you share with yours. If this is the case, I encourage you to continue to keep close your family ties so that they may help you to build and live your best life.

On the other hand, you may be reading this right now and can't even remember what your mother's voice sounds like. Perhaps you've never known your father because he left before you were born. Maybe you grew up in an abusive household and the concept of a loving and connected family is as phony to you as a three-dollar bill.

If this is the case, I support you in reconsidering the popular proverbs mentioned at the beginning of this chapter. In fact, I urge you to look to a different proverb that comes directly from the Bible: "There is a friend that sticks closer than a brother." This debunks the notion that blood is always thicker than water. The reality is, blood may be thicker than water, but love is greater than anything!

Take this knowledge and apply it to your current situation, whatever it is. Assess which family members support you unconditionally, and then hold on to them tightly. Make it your priority to let them know how much you appreciate having them in your life. Support them in their ventures and watch as you continue to be blessed in yours.

Now assess which family members no longer belong in your inventory. The ones who keep coming in and out of your life at their convenience. The ones who've abandoned you or abused you, stolen from you or embarrassed you. It's time to take them off your roster. Just because they share your last name, they are not automatically entitled to a place in your life.

How can you soar among eagles if your family has kept you trapped on the ground for so long? By allowing yourself to remain this way, you're actually becoming the one to blame for your misery. You can't change the family hurts inflicted on you in the past. But, if you want to live your best life right now, you must not allow for further harm to be done. Walk away with your pride and dignity knowing that your best life is waiting for you right around the corner.

CHAPTER NINE

Assess Your Better Half

In a 1989 *TIME* magazine interview, Mother Teresa said, "The hunger for love is much more difficult to remove than the hunger for bread."

As with most things said by Mother Teresa, these words echo as true today as they did then. In fact, I believe they will ring true in our hearts and in our minds forever.

The simple fact is, love is the greatest gift we've been given. I truly believe, even if some individuals won't admit it, that we all feel a deep longing to give love and to receive love. To me, that is what we were put on this Earth to do – to love and to be loved.

It's important to note that there are different types of love. We can look to the Ancient Greek explanation that there are four types including unconditional love, platonic or friendly love, family love, and passionate or romantic love. There's a general understanding that in order for love to last in our lives, we must find a balance and harmony between all of these areas.

To talk about passionate or romantic love is to talk about *relationships*. We've all been in one, are currently in one or want to be in one. Relationships, like love, make the world go 'round.

Traditionally, our society has always placed an enormous focus on romantic relationships. It's always been a socially accepted norm to find and marry a partner, have some children and grow old together. Yet, as time and generations have passed, things seem to have changed somewhere along the way. Divorce rates are climbing and unhappiness in love now seems to be the norm.

Granted, our world is a different place now more than ever before. Single men and women have greater opportunities to find success on their own terms. The traditional "relationship" is not so easily defined. Regardless of these facts, so many of us still want a lifelong partner to share in our lives. When our relationships are going well, our lives seem to be going well. But when these relationships fail, our world comes tumbling down around us.

Right now, I want you to assess your current loving relationship. Think about your boyfriend, girlfriend, fiancé, husband or wife. Are you smiling? Do you feel a sense of peace and happiness? Or do you feel agitated, aggravated or maybe even jealous? Do you feel unsure about the future? Are you thinking about something your loved one has done to you in the past that you still have not been able to forgive?

If you experience any type of ill feelings toward your loved one when you think about him or her, you truly need to assess your relationship. I'm not talking about a minor irritation like your husband leaving the toilet seat up all of the time. I'm not talking about the disagreement you had with your girlfriend because she took too long getting ready for the day. I'm talking about real, painful and ongoing hurts in your relationships – issues that keep coming up whenever you fight, issues that cause you to go mad with anger or jealousy.

We all know someone who has been cheated on, treated poorly or even abused by a partner. Maybe you are that someone. Ever notice that this person keeps going back to try again? Worse yet, that the person keeps going back only to be treated the same way each and every single time?

I have spent hours on the phone with a friend of mine who allows her "boyfriend," for lack of a better term, to treat her this way. Each time he treats her poorly, she vows to never allow him back in her life again. Low and behold, she gives in and the cycle is repeated. The same results for doing the same thing over and over again. To expect anything else would be insanity, but she justifies her actions by claiming that "love" makes people do crazy things.

The truth is, this is *not* love. As my motivational friend and mentor Tony Gaskins Jr. always says, "Love doesn't hurt, it heals." Think about this for a moment. If you are in a relationship that is hurting you, it is not love. By allowing someone to continue to cheat on you, treat you poorly and abuse you, you are just as responsible for the pain in your life as the person who is inflicting it. This is uncomfortable to think about, but it's the truth.

Imagine yourself going to a restaurant and ordering off the menu. It is most often the case that whatever you select from the menu is what the server will bring to you. You don't typically walk into an establishment and have random things brought to you that you didn't order.

Your life is like going to a restaurant and ordering off the menu. Whoever and whatever you order for your life is what's going to be delivered to your table. How can you continue to order a woman who cheats on you and be surprised every time she does it? How can you continue to order a man who abuses you and then act stunned when he's the one who shows up to your table?

So many people try to victimize themselves. They run around claiming that they are "unlucky in love." They try to make everyone around them think it's the universe's fault that they are still alone and single or in toxic relationships. They claim that it's everyone's fault but their own.

I ask you, what have you ordered for your life? If what you've ordered is not what you thought it would be, send it back and do not order it again. You may forever in your life have some type of reminder of your past mistakes, but you can keep yourself from ordering the same mistakes again in your future.

When you decide to let someone go, you may find that he or she has moved on to someone else and is now happy in that relationship. She may have stopped cheating or he may have stopped being emotionally abusive. Don't be alarmed at this; it has nothing to do with you.

You must realize that just because a person is a certain way with you doesn't mean that he or she will be that way with someone else. Your ex's love language with you was toxic because the relationship wasn't meant to be. This doesn't mean that he or she is going to be toxic for a new partner down the road.

With that said, you may find that every single one of your relationships are crumbling because of the same issue. If this is the case, it may be something on your end that needs work. We all need to better ourselves and seek ways to improve the way we love others. I have found that the best way to do this is to first love yourself. If you are not happy with your own life, your own appearance or your own hopes and dreams, you absolutely will not be able to love someone else.

Another common error we make in relationships is that we try to love people the way *we* want to be loved. This does not lead to romantic success. Instead, love a person the way *he* or *she* needs to be loved. A lot of relationships crumble because we give our partners what we *think* they want rather than what they *actually* need. Mind-reading has no place in any relationship; open lines of communication are a must.

There are so many facets to what make a good, loving relationship work. If you simply can't seem to get things right, it's a great idea to seek a life coach who specializes in relation- ships. By consulting with a motivational and objective friend, you will likely get clarity about your past relationships and find new ways to improve upon them in the future. Even if you are in a loving and lasting relationship, a life coach can help you bring it to the next level. Within each of us in an infinite ability to love and to be loved. Sometimes we all need a reminder of how to let this love show.

It is time to assess your better half. If he or she is not making your life *better*, you must force yourself to face some uncomfortable truths. If it's something you are doing that's hurting your relationships, work on it. If it's something your partner is doing, and continues to do, it's time to move on.

Our lives are enriched by the harmony we experience with different types of love. You cannot live your *best life* if the *love of your life* is hurting you and not helping you. What you accept, you can expect. Accept nothing but the greatest of love and you can expect to have it. You can expect your best life.

PART
IV

Act Now

CHAPTER TEN

Declutter Your Life

Having the right mindset is only one half of the journey to living your best life. Once you've put your mind in the right place, have chosen the right attitude and have taken inventory of your relationships, it's time to put your best life into action. It's time to stop waiting for good things to happen to you. Go out and make them happen!

Anytime you venture out to try something new, there is a certain level of uncertainty or anxiety that will try to overtake you. This is human nature. You are not alone in feeling this way. In order to live your best life, though, you must push past these feelings and dare to accomplish what you have set out to do.

Action in the face of fear is what living your best life is all about. This is also what it means to have courage or to be brave. Bravery is not the absence of fear but confidently pushing forward even when you are fearful. If you want to discover new shores, you absolutely must lose sight of the ones to which you have always been accustomed.

When I got my break in the entertainment industry, it wasn't because of luck or natural talent or ability. It was because I pushed forward with my plan even though I was scared out of my mind. Truthfully, I had very little idea what I was doing when organizing my first Hollywood event. It could have been a disaster in the making, but I refused to sit back and fail because of a lack of trying. By going for it in the face of my fear, I achieved success and discovered a new passion in my life that continues to burn bright. Had I not acted upon my desire to be a promoter, I would still be wondering what it feels like to share the stage with some of Daytime television's greatest stars.

If you're feeling stuck and can't seem to push yourself to the level of greatness that you've been aspiring to reach, it's likely time for you to declutter your life. So often we sit stagnant while our destiny remains unfulfilled. To me, the number one destiny-killer is the clutter that exists in your life. If you want to take action toward fulfilling your dreams, you must get rid of all the clutter that has overtaken your world.

Clutter takes several forms. It can be negative thoughts that creep into your mind or negative people that find their way into your life. Clutter can also take shape in your life in a very physical way. If you hold on to old clothing, old textbooks or old love letters, you are a victim of clutter. If you buy tons of things because they're on sale but don't ever use them, you are a victim of clutter. The list goes on. Having clutter in your life simply means holding on to anything that is no longer of use to you or bettering your life in any particular way.

If you knew me growing up, you would know that I was the worst when it came to holding on to clutter. My mom would always say I was just like my grandpa Rocco (whom I've never met) in the way that he loved to keep everything. You name it, he kept it. I was the same way. I kept old clothes, old toys, old school work – the list could stretch on for miles. For years, my entire life was stored away and preserved in a series of labelled cardboard boxes.

To be honest, my need to keep everything got very severe and debilitating. At one point in my life, I would buy two copies of almost everything I purchased, no matter what it was. One to use and enjoy, the other to store for the future. It sounds crazy but it's true. I literally had doubles of every single thing I purchased, minus grocery and food items. A close friend of mine still affectionately calls me "Double Mar" as that is what I was always known to do – own double copies of everything.

You could imagine the amount of clutter that this

caused in my life. Physically, at first, but then mentally. Looking at all of my junk from the past would actually cause me to lapse into deep periods of nostalgia. I would spend hours on end staring at old pictures. I'd spend a weekend trying to fix old toys that I played with when I was 5-years-old. I'd often long for the way things used to be and spend so much of my energy re-living dreams and ambitions that had already been fulfilled. I became stuck. Stagnant. I stopped growing.

Rid yourself right now of anything that is cluttering your world. If it's taking up space in your house, it's taking up space in your mind. Having my first yard sale, though it was an arduous task, allowed me to finally say farewell to so much of the baggage I had been carrying with me throughout my life. I urge you to do the same. If you don't have time to sell your clutter, give it away for free. There are a lot of organizations that would gladly take your used items and donate them to charity. It doesn't matter how you get rid of your clutter, just make sure that the junk is gone for good.

Who you are right now is not defined by the physical reminders of your past. You do not need old letters to remember the first time you were in love. You do not need old silverware to remind you of the first home you ever had. You do not need old toys to remind you of your great childhood.

Stop spending so much time and energy on things that

are no longer relevant to your purpose. If you spend your time consumed by the way things *were*, you will never find the energy to enjoy the way things *are*. When you live in the moment, you allow yourself an open mind to guide you toward your destiny. What are you waiting for? Declutter your world right now and allow your best life to unfold.

CHAPTER ELEVEN

Live to Serve

If you want to live your best life, there's no more meaningful way to do so than by helping others to live theirs. As a matter of fact, the best way to get anything you want in life is to first give it away.

If you want to make money, help someone else make money. If you want to be happy, help someone else be happy. Whatever it is that your heart desires, give it away freely and lovingly to others, and then watch as it flows abundantly back into your life.

We often hear, "What goes around comes around." Whether or not you believe in karma, you must understand the truth that is rooted in this phrase. What you give to others will come back to you. This has nothing to do with black magic or universal pull. It's just a matter of common sense. How others treat you is directly related to how you treat them. Love and be loved. Serve and be served. This is how the world works.

I recall being in Los Angeles several years ago with my brother-in-law Steve to visit our friend Mike. The three of us were on our way to dinner but first had to stop at a grocery store so that Mike could wire fifty dollars to a friend who was in a tight spot. I remember being very hungry and feeling slightly inconvenienced. Mike was insistent, though, that he get the money to his friend as soon as possible. "A friend in need," was all he said.

Let it be known that Mike is genuinely a caring and giving guy. He knew he was making us late for dinner, but he put first the immediate need of a friend without expecting anything in return. Instead of seeing his friend's need as an inconvenience, Mike gave openly and freely of his time and money.

Later that evening, Mike drove us back to our hotel but was feeling a little too tired to drive back to his place. He decided to book a room so he could crash for the night and head back in the morning. Low and behold, though this hotel was notorious for charging some pretty strict rates, Mike went to the counter and was offered a discount of sixty dollars off his room. He looked at me and smiled. He didn't need to say anything; I knew what his smirk was hinting at. "See, Mario, I gave away fifty bucks today, and now I've gotten even more back in return."

I'm not saying that when you give something away

you're going to immediately reap a greater return. I'm not even suggesting that karma or universal pull will take care of you to ensure that you get back double of whatever you give to others. What I am saying, though, is that the way you treat others will naturally shine through in your day-to-day interactions. People you meet will be enthralled by your giving and generous spirit. In return, they will feel naturally inclined to give back to you. This is why good givers make great getters!

Of course, being of service to others isn't a matter of, "You scratch my back and I'll scratch yours." Service is about assessing what you can give to others and then giving of it freely. If you are in a position to help others financially, do so. You may not have a lot of money but, instead, you have a lot of wisdom to impart on others. Wherever you are in your current situation, it is imperative that you are sharing your gifts with others. By bettering the life of someone else, your life will be better.

I have a friend who works for a school board where teachers create their own lesson plans and keep them hidden from their colleagues. It's practically a sin to ask a co-worker for help. These individuals seem to follow the motto, "You do you and I'll do me." In the school board for which I work, teachers are the exact opposite. We give freely of our resources and materials. Sure, I may spend a lot of time creating a certain unit plan or series of lessons for my students, but I share my ideas freely with my co-workers and appreciate that they do the same. The ultimate goal is to reach our students to the best of our abilities. Personal and professional egos have no place. We serve one another so that we may be served and continue to serve.

In your career, you likely know people who are secretive and keep their work to themselves so that they may get all the credit. You also probably know people who are the exact opposite, who give of their time and energy to improve the work of everyone around them. Ask yourself the question, "Which of these types do I prefer to work with?" It's an obvious choice. Now ask yourself, "Which of these types am I?"

When you live to serve others, whether at work, at home, amongst friends or even strangers, you are putting yourself in a position to be served. By giving of yourself, you are not taking away anything from your life. As the proverb goes, "A candle loses nothing by lighting another candle." Your light does not diminish when you let it shine on others.

A lot of people spend the majority of their lives trying to figure out why they're here. So many ask, "What is the meaning of life?" and expect an answer to someday magically fall out of the sky. I truly believe that the answer is already here and that it's rooted in what we do during our time on Earth.

Simply put, you are here to love and to share your gifts with the world. You have been put on God's green Earth so that you can serve others. When you connect your purpose in life to service, you will quickly see that they are one in the same. Your purpose *is* service.

What are you doing in your life right now to serve others? If you can't answer this question, you're probably one of the people who constantly wonder about the meaning of life. I urge you, get to giving right now! Give freely and lovingly. Give to others anything you can. If giving to other people won't hurt your life but it will help theirs, do it. I promise you, an abundance of blessings and favor are in your forecast. Even though you will give to others with a selfless attitude, you can expect great things in return. Live in service and purpose and watch as your best life gets even better!

CHAPTER TWELVE

Go Where You're Celebrated

In a perfect world, we would all get along and encourage one another on our paths to fulfilling greatness. I know that you have a high desire to travel such a path. You are a strong-willed and ambitious person with unlimited potential to live the life you have always imagined.

The problem is, not everyone in your world will feel the same way you do. In fact, many people that you will meet and work with in your lifetime are the exact opposite of you. They appear to have no hopes, no dreams and no ambitions for a better future. Part of their life's purpose may even seem to be sucking the purpose out of yours.

Know this – nobody is born with a broken soul. Souls are broken along the way. The people in your life who are downtrodden, miserable or even downright angry did not enter the world like that. Instead, they learned these behaviors from all of the downtrodden, miserable and angry people that have surrounded them. Now that they are miserable, they know how to do nothing else but make your life miserable, too.

Misery *loves* company. Hurt people *hurt* people. Look at it any way you want. It's all the same way of saying that you need to be careful of anyone who will try to belittle your dreams. When people are feeling down about their own lives, they will naturally try and suck you into feeling down about yours.

As a teacher, I see this sort of behavior all the time. It seems to inherently exist with some children. The media likes to call it "bullying." I see it more as the spreading of misery. You can probably remember the mean kids who went to school with you. Some loved to push and shove; the majority got their kicks by calling people names or laughing at others. Today, this problem is trickier than ever with the insurgence of social media and smartphones.

Studies consistently show that these children who push others around were once, themselves, victims. They may come from broken homes where they learned that it's okay to treat others poorly. They may have learned these negative behaviors from being picked on by their peers.

I teach my students the same thing that most parents teach their children — if you're being surrounded by people who make your life miserable, stick up for yourself by walking away. You don't fight fire with fire; you fight fire with water. As adults, we need to make sure that we are teaching ourselves the same things we try to teach our children.

In my life, I have learned to go where I'm celebrated and not just tolerated. It is not enough to exist in life with the people around you. You must live your life to its fullest purpose. If you want to live your best life, you absolutely have no time to waste on others who are bullying you, putting you down, ignoring you and sucking the wind out of your sails.

Too often, we focus the majority of our time on dodging people who we think are bad for us but who really have no bearing on our lives. The ones you truly need to be careful around are the toxic people who surround you daily. These individuals often come across as quite innocent and harmless. The co-workers who gossip at the water cooler. The friends who only ever talk about themselves. The family members who never ask you how your day was. These people don't directly cause you any problems, but they certainly are not helping your life in any way, either.

By allowing yourself to be surrounded by people like this, you are going where you are *tolerated*. Instead, live your best life by learning to go where you are *celebrated*. Practice loving everyone and everything at all times, but only surround yourself with people who better your life. You can choose to hang around stagnant people and keep your life at a standstill, or you can choose to hang with those who will lift you up. Choosing the latter means choosing to go where you are celebrated.

Mark Twain once said, "Keep away from people who try to belittle your ambitions. Small people always do that, but the really great make you feel that you, too, can become great." There is real value in having friends and family who can celebrate your accomplishments. When we support one another in our victories, we are paving the way for more to happen. Never underestimate the power of a pat on the back. Sometimes, it's all we need to continue to strive forward.

If the people in your life are not celebrating you, love them anyway but steer clear of their path. It's just a matter of time until they start to bring you down. When people refuse to celebrate you, they're showing their true colors. What they're really saying is, "We're ignoring your accomplishments because we haven't done anything with our own lives." Little do they realize the power of celebrating others. When you are celebrated, you are pushed forward to new levels of greatness. When you celebrate others, you still push yourself toward new levels of greatness. Celebrating with one another is a win-win situation for everyone involved.

Recognize that you are as good as the company you

keep. If you want to remain a chicken pecking on the ground for the rest of your life, keep the company of others who do nothing except tolerate you. But if you want to soar with eagles, surround yourself with other uplifting individuals who inspire you and who celebrate your life. In doing so, you will fly to new heights and truly establish the best life that's been created for you.

PART

V

The Secret to Success

CHAPTER THIRTEEN
Love What You Do

I want to introduce you to two very close friends of mine.

Meet Tim. Tim is 45-years-old. He's a specialist physician at one of the largest hospitals in North America. He works crazy hours and is paid very well for his duties. In a quiet year, he makes approximately half-a-million dollars. His house is massive and situated on the waterfront. He drives the best car and wears the finest clothes. Tim is also recognized in countless magazines around the world as being a leading physician at the cutting edge of his field. He's a borderline celebrity.

Meet Fred. Fred is also 45-years-old. He's a service clerk at the local grocery store where he's worked since dropping out of college when he was 18. Fred works full-time during the week with weekends off. In an average year, he makes twenty-thousand dollars. He's driven the same Pontiac Sunfire since 1999 and shops at Wal-Mart for the latest deal on jeans.

Fred's greatest accomplishment was being named Employee of the Year several years ago.

Who would you say is the greater success story – Tim or Fred? Before you answer, allow me to let you in on a few more details.

Tim's been devastated for the last eight years since his wife and children left him. He never wanted to get sucked in by his work yet somehow found himself in a position where he was always at the hospital and never with his family. Since he's been living alone, he shows up miserable to the office every day. Tim hates his work.

Fred's job at the grocery store hasn't allowed him to buy his wife or children the finer things in life, but he loves having weekends off to rest with his family. During the week, he looks forward to chatting with his loyal customers and takes great pride in perfectly packing their groceries. Fred loves his work.

Let me ask you again – who is the greater success story? Now that we have more pieces to the puzzle, you're more likely to say that Fred is the greater success story because he loves what he does.

And there you have it – the secret to success.

It's sort of anti-climactic, isn't it? I wish I could make it more exciting for you, but this "secret" that has evaded the masses for so long is really just a straightforward fact that we all inherently know.

Without a shadow of a doubt, the true secret to success is to love what you're doing. You also need to define what success means to you. In my case, I happen to love teaching and I'm passionate about it. I love being creative while helping others and it just happens to also be my job, so that's a great day for me.

Take a long, hard look at your life and ask yourself, "Am I doing what I have always wanted to do? Am I living out my blueprint for success?" This is *your* success that we're talking about. It's got to be *your* life and *your* dream if you can truly say that you are successful.

In life, sometimes people will send us down a path other than what we originally intended for ourselves. Maybe your mom forced you to go to university so that you could become a lawyer or a dentist. Perhaps your spouse is pressuring you to stick with your dead-end job because it helps pay the bills.

If this is the case in your life, I encourage you to remember that success is defined by you and only you. You've got to know what it is that you want to succeed at in order to be successful with it. Now is the time to take control of your life. Take the wheel and drive confidently down the road you have always wanted to travel.

When I decided to take the wheel and head toward fulfilling my dream of working with stars of Daytime television, I had a very clear goal in mind. I defined success according to my own terms so that I could meaningfully chase after it and eventually become it. The road wasn't clearly mapped out for me; I went for it anyway. Sometimes you have to throw practicality out the window, or you may spend the rest of your life kicking yourself that you never had the guts to take the chance. Define your success and then become it. When you have a clear picture of your dream, you are more likely to not only succeed in it but to also love every step along the way.

As clearly as you foresee your future, recognize that things may not turn out to be exactly what you expected. This is okay as long as you truly love what you're doing. For me, working in the entertainment industry has been everything I wanted it to be but nothing like I dreamed it would be. Like anything in life, it's what you make of it that becomes your reality. As long as a true passion exists for what you do, you are doing it well.

When you make that leap toward your dream, don't worry if you feel anxious about making your way through uncharted territory. Remember, bravery is not the absence of fear but confidently pushing forward even when you are fearful. Dare to be brave. If you love what you are doing, you will find a way to get it done. Believe me, your passion and love for what you do will give you a renewed sense of energy and strength. Your energy and strength, rooted in your success, will immerse you into your best life.

CHAPTER FOURTEEN
Don't Give Away Your Power

When you can truly say that you love what you do, you absolutely have no need to compare yourself to what others are doing. Being successful means being comfortable in your achievements. It means knowing who you are, what you stand for and where you intend to go next. Anytime you allow yourself to doubt your purpose or allow others to belittle what you have accomplished, you are giving away your power.

Having power means focusing on the things you can control. During any given day, there are a lot of people who will pose as inconveniences to you. At any given time, your situation can change because of an accident or unforeseen circumstance. You cannot control these people or these situations. What you can control, however, is the way in which you react and adapt to them.

It's been said that life is 10% what happens to you and 90% how you react to it. Understand that this is the truth. By knowing that your reactions are what ultimately shape your world, you are setting yourself up for the best life you could ever imagine. What happens to you in your life is not going to dictate your success. Your ability to roll with the changes is what will place you at a higher level than most. Be flexible on a day-to-day basis. Bend, don't break. Choose to react with positivity whenever possible.

Let's say you're running late for work and are stuck in a traffic jam. You can honk your horn all you want and tailgate the car in front of you, but your car still isn't moving. You can curse and slam your hands down on your wheel. You can bite your lip and feel like screaming at the top of your lungs, but that still won't get you to your job on time. All that you have essentially done is give an inanimate thing like traffic the ability to completely ruin your day. You've raised your blood pressure and put yourself in a bad mood. You have given away your power.

Instead, the next time you're stuck in traffic, quietly say to yourself, "This is something I cannot control. I'm going to remain calm even though I feel anxious about getting to work on time. The important thing is that I have a job to go to. I'm thankful for this moment. It's where I'm supposed to be."

Speaking of your job, I want you to think right now about the most irritating and aggravating co-workers you've ever had. Spending Monday to Friday with people can really make you want to pull their hair out, especially if they're obnoxious or negative individuals. They boil your blood all day until you finally snap and say, "You make me so mad!" But what you've actually said to them is, "Here, have my power."

Difficult people and aggravating situations are inevitable. There's no such thing as a perfect life. Show me a man who says his life is perfect and I will, indeed, show you a liar. All of our lives are filled with inconvenient people and difficult situations. We are constantly surrounded by others. No man is an island.

It's impossible to entirely prevent uncomfortable people and circumstances from creeping up into your world. You can, however, dictate how you will respond to these discomforts. When people get under your skin, stop thinking that you can set them straight or teach them a lesson. It is not your duty to try to change people. You need to change your attitude.

When you are faced with difficult people or uncomfortable situations, always remember that you have a conscious choice to make. By purposely choosing to rise above the people and situations that are bringing you down, you have chosen to hold on to your power. This is absolutely mandatory if you truly wish to live your best life.

Whether I'm onstage in front of hundreds of people,

in a classroom standing before dozens of students or just talking with a complete stranger, I will never give away my power. I know who I am. I'm comfortable with where I've been in life and where I'm heading. Even if certain things come up that may irritate or bother me, I won't give away my power.

I love my power. Why would I give it away?

The way I see it, when you're comfortable in your own skin and secure with your own life, you will never find yourself in a position to give away your power. It's not even an option. It shouldn't matter if somebody else has more money than you. You shouldn't care if you don't have as many materialistic things as others. Don't let it bother you if your classmates think you're less attractive than your peers. Truly successful people do not compare themselves to those around them. Truly successful people never devalue themselves by giving others more value.

From now on, I want you to think of sandpaper every time you're confronted with a difficult person or uncomfortable situation. Just like a piece of sandpaper will take the rough edges off of anything it's rubbed against, these difficult people and situations will remove the rough edges off of you. By holding your head high in the face of adversity, you are holding on to your power. Not only that, you are actually becoming a better person because you are allowing all of your rough edges to be rubbed away.

Moving forward, I encourage you to keep a level head and to never give away your power. Remember that it is impossible to control all of your circumstances but mandatory to control your reactions to them. Trust that you are living a life of purpose and are successful in whatever you are doing. Nothing that anyone says or does can upset you or control you. You have the power to live your best life!

CHAPTER FIFTEEN

Realize Your Destiny

There's an idea out there that we are all destined for a particular lot in life. A particular job, a particular income, a particular set of circumstances. The average person will say that your destiny cannot be changed no matter what you do. I say that the average person is completely misinformed.

To assume that you're destined to live anything less than your best life is to assume that you have no purpose here on this Earth. When you say, "I'm not destined for greatness" you are actually saying, "I have no purpose." If you have ended up with a lackluster life it's because that's what you have falsely determined was meant for you.

When you were created, you weren't created by mistake. You are living and breathing at this very moment because you have a purpose to fulfill. You are meant to be here. But how your life looks right now is not the result of what's been predetermined for you. Your destiny is shaped by the choices you make, the chances you take and the company you keep. Stop listening to the negative people who will try to convince you otherwise.

There's always going to be a smart alec who says, "How do you control getting sick with cancer? Or getting killed in an automobile accident?" I'm not talking about these sorts of things. In life, there are circumstances we cannot control. But do you want to live with this helpless attitude? Do you really think you can enjoy your life along the way if all you're focused on is the end result of your physical time on Earth?

I'm talking about shaping your day-to-day life. To me, that's what your destiny is. Your destiny is what you are doing to live your best life *right now*. I'm not talking about end results. I'm talking about the journey along the way. The day-to-day things shape who you are, how you live and how you will be remembered.

If you think it's your destiny to be stuck in a dead-end marriage, think again. If you assume it's your destiny to work a minimum wage job your whole life, you've assumed wrong. If you can't see that it's your destiny to fulfill your heart's innermost desires, you are not looking hard enough.

My friend, I promise that you can shape your destiny. Most CEOs of *Fortune 500* companies do not just fall into their positions; they work their way to the top. They find a way to make it happen. Doctors and lawyers don't make the money they do because they "got lucky" with high paying jobs; they completed the necessary schooling. A mechanic who makes six figures does not just happen to have customers coming his way; he's proven himself through his solid work.

If you're not happy with your current salary or your current career, don't assume it's your destiny to stay there. Take the necessary steps to get to where you want to be. It's often our own mental barriers that keep us from doing what we want to do or being where we want to be. You might think, "I'm too old to go back to school" but, the reality is, you've just gotten too comfortable in your current situation. I urge you, right now, to take the steps needed to reshape your dreams and to rebuild your destiny. Make it happen in your life.

Whatever you do, don't blame your lack of success on being dealt a bad hand. I hear it all the time. "Other people are more talented than I am" or "I don't have the necessary skills to be successful." These are all excuses made by lazy people who choose to settle for mediocrity.

I recall watching an interview several years ago with Will Smith, arguably one of the most successful actors and celebrity icons of this generation. He spoke very clearly about how people need to recognize the difference between talent and skill in order to achieve their dreams. "Talent you have naturally," he said. "Skill is only developed by hours and hours and hours of beating on your craft."

Recognize that the talents and gifts needed to achieve your destiny are already inside of you. They've been there all along. These gifts are yours and yours alone. To fulfill your destiny, you must practice using your gifts in order to develop the necessary skills to achieve success. It is only through countless hours of developing your skills that you can then apply them to attaining your best life.

An old motivational friend of mine once said, "If it isn't rough, it isn't right." These seven words have changed my life; let them change yours. Recognize that there is a real message in the struggle. If something is coming easily to you, it's likely something that won't last or something that won't better your life in the long run. Anything that will truly lead you to your best life will indeed take time, energy and an unwavering passion to achieve. It may be rough, but it's all right!

Don't even let financial issues stop you along the way. Many of us assume that if we just had some more money, we could accomplish greater things. This is completely false. Some of the richest people I know aren't fulfilling their destinies. They have all the money in the world but haven't discovered their true purpose. They are bored with their lives. On the other hand, some of the most successful people with whom I've worked have come from financially unstable situations. They started with not a penny to their name but found a way to get it done. We often hear, "Where there's a will, there's a way." Truer words have never been spoken. Trust in this and go for it!

Put the work in and accept nothing less than the best from yourself and the people around you. What you accept in your life is what you can expect in your life. Set the bar high and your destiny will become more clear. As you push forward with purpose, your destiny will unveil itself in all of its glory.

Move toward the life you've always wanted but understand that not everyone can come with you. In a perfect world, all of your friends and family would climb by your side to the top of the mountain. The unfortunate truth is this – not everyone you know has the same drive to climb the same mountain. Not everyone will invest in themselves the same way you have invested in yourself. In these cases, you must go ahead and climb without them.

Not everyone will understand what you're doing as you create your destiny and live the life you've always imagined. You can try to help others comprehend your dream but you can't force them to understand. Some people won't grasp what you're doing because it's not for them. Don't sweat it. If you try to take them with you, they will only drag you down.

As you undertake this attitude of excellence, some people around you will feel like you've rubbed them the wrong way. When people watch you set the bar high, some will accuse you of being difficult. When people see that you only accept the best, some will accuse you of being selfish. As people watch you shape your destiny and share your accomplishments with the world, some will accuse you of bragging.

In contrast, some people around you will genuinely cheer for your every move. They will support you whole-heartedly. They will never question, or be critical of, any of the work that you're doing.

Be warned – if you truly want to live your best life, you cannot spend too much of your time focusing on either the negative *or* positive feedback that you will undoubtedly receive. Both types can be dangerous and limit your overall perception of reality. Remember, your success is defined by you and you alone. Keep pressing forward with your head held high and trust that you're living a successful life full of purpose. There's no time to listen to what everyone says about you. Maintain the attitude that what other people think of you is absolutely none of your business! This is not arrogance; it's destiny.

It is your best life.

DON'T JUST SETTLE FOR A GOOD LIFE
Live Your Best Life

DEEP INSIDE OF YOU is a natural gift that's waiting to be unleashed. A gift that will transform your good life into your best life.

By reading this book, you have taken the first step in bringing your purpose to a whole new level. Now you have the opportunity to work one-on-one with Mario for personalized results that will see you dominating in your field!

Visit mariorocchetta.com today to get started.

YOUR BEST LIFE AWAITS.

27286836R10065

Made in the USA
Charleston, SC
07 March 2014